This book presented to:

_____

By:

_____

On:

_____

Best-Loved Christmas Stories

CONCORDIA PUBLISHING HOUSE • SAINT LOUIS

Arch® Books
Published 2014 by Concordia Publishing House
3558 S. Jefferson Ave., St. Louis, MO 63118-3968
1-800-325-3040 • www.cph.org

Mary's Christmas Story © 1996 Concordia Publishing House.

Joseph's Christmas Story © 2002 Concordia Publishing House.

Baby Jesus Is Born © 1996, revised 2004 Concordia Publishing House.

The Shepherds Shook in Their Shoes © 2010 Concordia Publishing House.

Star of Wonder © 2005 Concordia Publishing House.

My Merry Christmas Arch Book © 1995 Concordia Publishing House.

All rights reserved. No part of this publication may be reproduced, stored in a retrieval system, or transmitted, in any form or by any means, electronic, mechanical, photocopying, recording, or otherwise, without the prior written permission of Concordia Publishing House.

Scripture quotation from The ESV Bible® (Holy Bible, English Standard Version®), copyright © 2001 by Crossway Bibles, a publishing ministry of Good News Publishers. Used by permission. All rights reserved.

Manufactured in Shenzhen, China/55760/300495

Table of Contents

Mary's Christmas Story	7
Joseph's Christmas Story	23
Baby Jesus Is Born	39
The Shepherds Shook in Their Shoes	55
The Star of Wonder	71
My Merry Christmas Arch Book	87

Dear Parents,

    Reindeer, Santa, snowmen, presents, and parties . . . this time of year brings such a jumble of noise and sights that the true reasons we celebrate may be lost in the confusion.

    This collection of Arch Books was chosen to teach today's children about the real events of the first Christmas. Beginning with the angel's message to Mary and ending with the child's own life, these stories provide biblical context so you can help expand your child's understanding of our Savior's birth and what it means to us today.

    As you read this book, talk about the whys of Christmas—our need for a Savior, God's promise fulfilled through that special baby, and the gifts of forgiveness and salvation He brings. Then talk

about how we know that Jesus is God's Son and our Savior—a wisdom that comes from faith as a gift from the Holy Spirit.

The gift of a Savior. The gift of faith in Him. These are the real reasons we celebrate.

May God bless your family with a happy Christmas season and grant that you know the joy and peace of forgiveness and salvation through the baby born at Christmas.

To Him be the glory!
The editor

Mary's Christmas Story

Luke 1:26–56
Luke 2:1–20 for children

Written by Teresa Olive
Illustrated by Nancy Munger

Young Mary lived in Nazareth, a town in Galilee.
She was a girl who tried to serve the Lord most faithfully.
As Mary sat quietly in her home one night,
The angel Gabriel appeared, shining oh so bright!

"Greetings!" said Gabriel. "You're favored by the Lord!"
Mary felt afraid and trembled at his words.
But the angel gently said, "Mary, do not fear.
God is very pleased with you, and He sent me here.

"You will have a baby named Jesus, God's own Son.
He will sit on David's throne, ruling everyone."
Mary did not understand. She asked, "How can this be?
I am still a virgin. I'm not married yet, you see."

Gabriel said, "God Himself will cause you to conceive.
Nothing is impossible with God—you may believe!
Your relative, Elizabeth, who is old and worn,
Is finally a mother—her child will soon be born."

"I am my good Lord's servant," Mary then did say.
"May your words all happen as you have said today."
Then Mary went on a journey far from Nazareth.
When she saw her cousin's home, she cried, "Elizabeth!"

As Mary spoke, Elizabeth felt her baby boy
Leaping high within her womb, jumping up with joy!
Elizabeth knew right away that Mary was the one
God had chosen as the mother of His only Son.

Mary said, "The Mighty One has been so good to me,
And to all of Israel—He's come to set us free!"
Mary stayed there visiting until three months were gone.
Then Elizabeth gave birth to a son named John.

And then King Caesar issued this command:
"A census will be taken throughout all the land."
So Mary and Joseph had to pack and travel down
To Bethlehem, since it was Joseph's family's town.

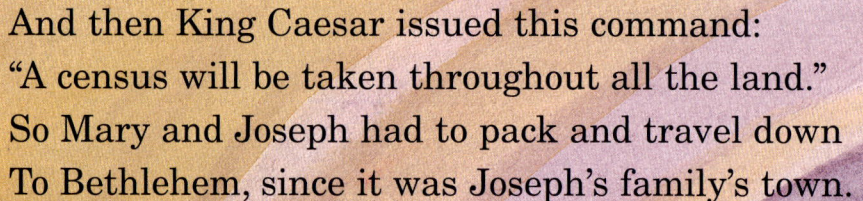

When at last they arrived in tiny Bethlehem,
Every room was full—there was no room for them.
Finally, an innkeeper invited them to stay
In his barn where they could sleep on the oxen's hay.

Soon the time came for the baby to be born.
Mary swaddled Him in cloths so He was snug and warm.
There was no crib or cradle for baby Jesus' bed,
So Mary gently laid Him on the manger's hay instead.

As Mary gazed upon the face of her newborn Son,
Some shepherds came in saying, "He must be the one!"
Then they told their story: "We were watching sheep.
It was dark and quiet. We were half asleep.

"Suddenly, we saw a sight that jolted us awake—
An angel so glorious, our knees began to shake!
We fell down upon the ground, trembling in fear.
The angel said, 'Don't be afraid. I bring news of good cheer!

"'In the town of Bethlehem, God's Son was born today.
You will find Him wrapped in cloths in a manger's hay.'
Next we saw a host of angels lighting up the sky,
Lifting up their voices to the Lord Most High.

"They said, 'Glory to the Lord! Peace on earth to men!'
Then the angels vanished. It was dark again.
At first, we all just stood there, then we began to shout,
'Let us go to see the child the Lord told us about!'

"So we ran here and found it all just as the angel said—
Here's the Baby wrapped in cloths in His manger bed!"
Then the shepherds went around, telling everyone,
"God has sent a Savior—Jesus, His own Son!"

The people were amazed in crowded Bethlehem.
Could this baby be the King God had promised them?
Mary treasured all of this deep within her heart,
Thanking God for using her for such a loving part.

Dear Parents:

She was young, poor, and powerless. So why did God chose Mary to be the mother of His Son? Precisely because she was young, poor, and powerless, just as we are powerless in the face of sin and death. God worked through a humble young girl, a bewildered carpenter, a powerful Roman ruler, and many others to accomplish His plan of sending His Son to be our Savior.

Explain to your child that God continues to work through His people today, using us to share His love with others. Keep Christ's birthday foremost in your Christmas celebration this year. Purchase or make an Advent calendar or an Advent wreath. Ask God each day to prepare your hearts to celebrate the birth of His Son. Say a special prayer, or act out the Christmas story before opening your presents. Draft family pets to play the parts of animals in the stable!

Take some pictures of your special activities and keep them in a photo album. Look at them often with your child. "Ponder" God's goodness as Mary did and thank Him for His great love in sending His Son to be our Savior.

The Editor

The Story of Jesus' Birth
Matthew 1:18–24 and Luke 2:1–20 for children

Written by Nicole E. Dreyer
Illustrated by Len Ebert

Joseph was a carpenter
Who made things out of wood,
In a shop in Nazareth
Where business was quite good.

Joseph was to marry soon
A woman that he loved.
Mary was his dear one's name;
Both blessed by God above.

One day Joseph heard some news
That took him by surprise.
Mary was to have a child!
An angel had told her why:

"Your child," the angel Gabriel said,
"Will be the Son of God.
And you shall call Him Jesus."
But Joseph said, "That's odd."

27

So God then sent a special dream
To Joseph in the night.
"Do not fear," an angel said.
"Dear Joseph, it's all right."

Kind Joseph heard God's message.
That dream had changed his life.
So Joseph went to Mary
And took her for his wife.

Caesar was in charge back then.
He sent out this decree:
Everyone now owes a tax.
Go home to pay this fee.

So Joseph went to Bethlehem,
With Mary by his side.
Upon a soft brown donkey,
His pregnant wife did ride.

But when they came to David's town,
As Bethlehem was called,
All the rooms were filled up tight—
Except a manger stall.

Joseph went into that stall
And fixed a bed of hay.
Mary gratefully stretched out
To rest from their long day.

Suddenly the quiet night
Was filled with holy sound.
The animals were wide-awake
And gathered close around.

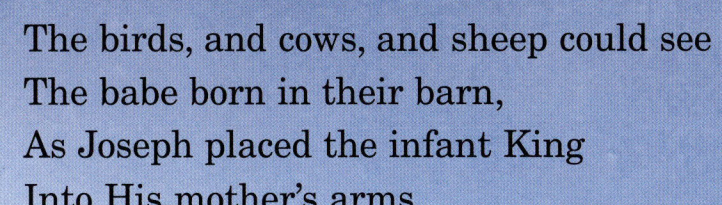

The birds, and cows, and sheep could see
The babe born in their barn,
As Joseph placed the infant King
Into His mother's arms.

And in the fields not far away,
Some shepherds were surprised
By angels bringing this Good News:
"The Savior has arrived!"

Into the town the shepherds went
To see this newborn one.
And when they came the shepherds said,
"We'd like to see your son."

But Joseph smiled and shook his head,
"This child is *God's* own Son—
Born today to save us all,
This Holy, Precious One."

The shepherds worshiped Jesus,
And we can worship too.
We'll kneel before the Savior
Who loves both me and you!

Dear Parents,

Too often Joseph is a forgotten character in the Christmas story. Think about his situation—the woman he is about to marry is going to have a baby, and he is not the father. Yet he trusts in God and obeys His command. Joseph accepts the responsibility and lovingly cares for Jesus as an earthly father.

The concept of being responsible is difficult to teach. One way to teach this concept is to "flip" the word around, indicating that responsibility is the "ability to respond." And we are blessed with the opportunity to respond to God's love for us in Jesus.

As a family, talk about ways you can be responsible and respond to God's love at the same time. Responsibility often means serving others. Thank God that He sent His Son to serve us as He took the punishment for our sins. Ask Him to help you accept responsibility with a servant heart.

The Editor

Baby Jesus is Born

Luke 2:1–20 for children

Written by Gloria A. Truitt   Illustrated by Kathy Mitter

Now in the town of Nazareth—
In the land of Galilee—
There lived a man named Joseph and
His promised wife-to-be.

Mary was the woman's name.
She was God's *favored one*,
For God had chosen her to be
The mother of His Son.

Caesar was the emperor
Two thousand years ago.
He told the folks he ruled to make
A trip quite hard and slow.

Joseph knew he had to heed
The emperor's decree,
So he and Mary set out from
The land of Galilee.

At last they came to Bethlehem,
A town of little size.
Now the streets were crowded, which
Was not a great surprise!

Joseph asked an innkeeper,
"Do you have room for two?"
"No," he said to Joseph, who
Then sighed, "What should I do?"

"I'm sorry," said the innkeeper,
"I really am unable
To provide a room for you …
But wait! I have a stable!"

Now, on that night our Lord was born
To save all folk on earth,
And that is why we still today
Observe His holy birth.

This baby was the promised King—
God's Son, this couple knew—
And so they named Him Jesus,
As God had told them to.

Some shepherds in a field nearby
Were tending to their flock,
When suddenly an angel came!
Imagine their great shock.

God's holy light surrounded them,
And they were so dismayed.
But then the angel of the Lord
Said, "Do not be afraid!

"I bring you good and joyous news.
For everyone this day,
A Savior has been born to you!
To Him, go find your way."

"You'll find this Baby
wrapped in cloths
And lying in a manger.
You'll know Him by these
signs and, so,
This Child won't be
a stranger."

They hurried off and found the Child,
Just as the angel said,
Inside a humble stable with
A manger for His bed.

They knelt beside this holy Child,
Then ran to spread the word,
Telling everyone they met
Of what they'd seen and heard.

Dear Parents,

Take time with your child during this busy Christmas season to worship the Christ Child, born to be your Savior. After reading this story, act it out, using the figures from your crèche set. Sing a Christmas hymn, such as "Away in a Manger." Assure your child of Jesus' great love—so great that He willingly exchanged His heavenly throne for a bed of straw and a cross.

Read the last page to your child again, and explain that the shepherds did not keep the good news of Jesus' birth to themselves. Invite friends or neighbors to your home for a Christmas devotion. Share with everyone around you the message that Jesus, God in the flesh, was born to bring the world forgiveness and eternal life.

The Editor

THE SHEPHERDS SHOOK IN THEIR SHOES

Luke 2 for Children

Written by Michelle Medlock Adams
Illustrated by Dana Regan

One night while shepherds did their jobs
And watched their sheep with care,
An angel of the Lord appeared
And gave them quite a scare!

The shepherds' hearts were full of fear.
They shook right in their shoes!
But then the angel called to them,
"Fear not, I've got good news!"

The shepherds didn't speak a word.
The sheep were quiet too.
They tried to "fear not" like he said,
But that was hard to do.

The angel was extremely bright—
Just like the noonday sun.
And when he spoke, his words of peace
Swept over everyone.

The shepherds listened carefully
To what he had to say.
Somehow they knew deep in their hearts,
It was a holy day.

The angel spoke of Jesus,
The One they'd waited for.
They moved a little closer in.
They wanted to hear more.

"For unto you this day is born
A Savior, Christ the Lord."
The angel spoke with strength and might.
He could not be ignored.

"He's in the City of David,"
They heard the angel say.
And then one shepherd said aloud,
"I must go there today!"

"And this shall be a sign to you,"
The angel boldly said.
"You'll find the babe in swaddling clothes
Upon a small straw bed."

With that, the angel spoke no more.
Then guess what filled the sky?
It was a multitude of hosts,
All hovering nearby!

The angels came to praise the Lord.
They all began to sing.
"Glory to God in the Highest!"
It was an awesome thing.

Their voices were quite beautiful.
They sang for quite a while:
"Peace on earth, good will toward men."
That made the shepherds smile.

Then suddenly, the angels left.
Their job that night was through.
They had announced the glorious news,
And now the shepherds knew.

"To Bethlehem!" one shepherd said.
"We have to go tonight!"
They longed to praise the King of kings
And see the holy sight.

The shepherds hurried on their way
Until they found the place.
They could not wait to see the Child
And gaze upon His face.

And then at last, they saw the Babe.
Their hearts were filled with joy.
They knew He was the precious Christ—
Not just a baby boy.

The shepherds left the holy place
And shared the news abroad.
They said, "We saw the King of kings!
We saw the Son of God!"

And some who heard the shepherds' news
Were puzzled at each word,
But all the shepherds praised the Lord
For what they'd seen and heard.

They knew they'd seen the King of kings.
They knew it in their heart.
They knew they'd never be the same.
They had a brand-new start.

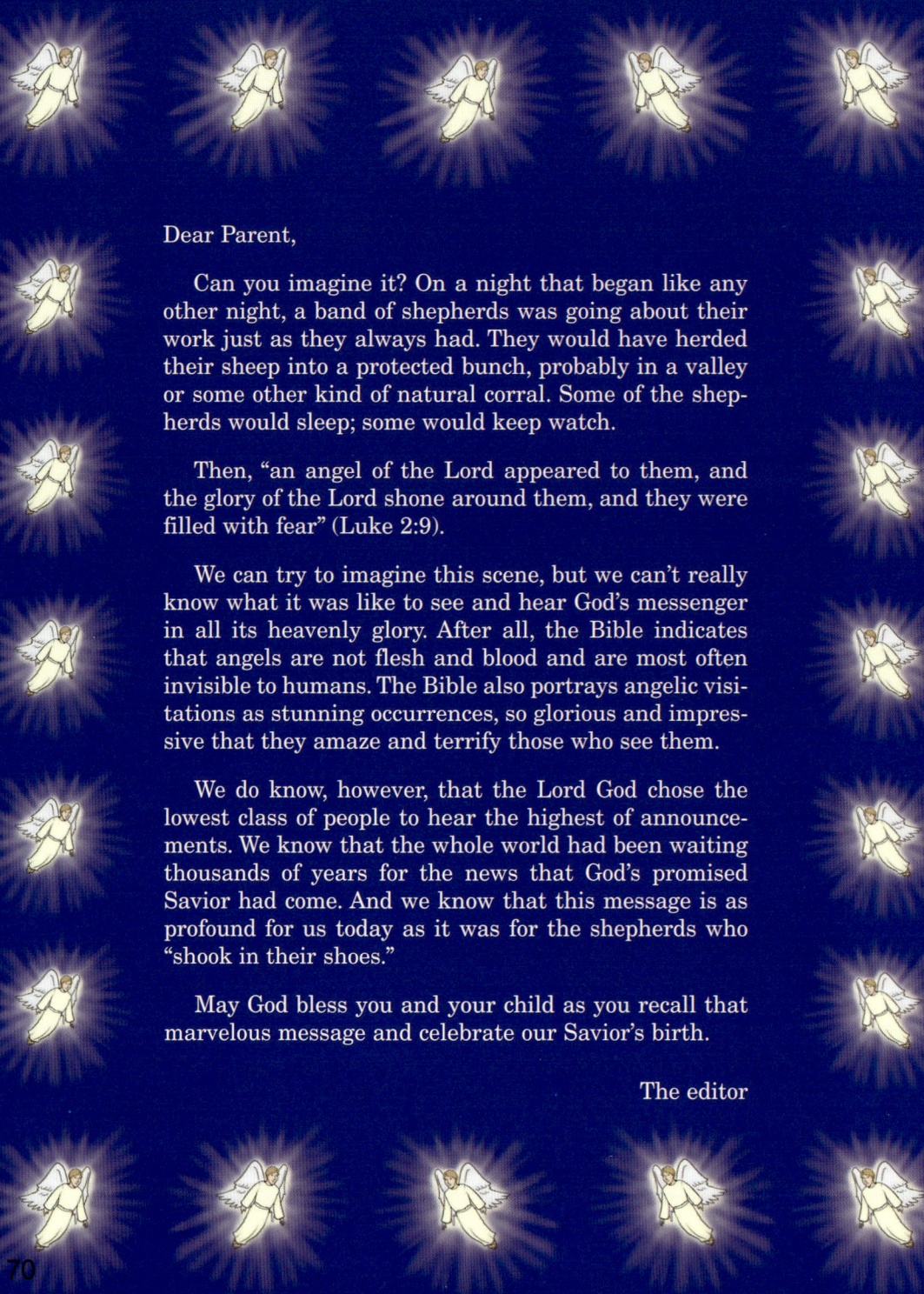

Dear Parent,

Can you imagine it? On a night that began like any other night, a band of shepherds was going about their work just as they always had. They would have herded their sheep into a protected bunch, probably in a valley or some other kind of natural corral. Some of the shepherds would sleep; some would keep watch.

Then, "an angel of the Lord appeared to them, and the glory of the Lord shone around them, and they were filled with fear" (Luke 2:9).

We can try to imagine this scene, but we can't really know what it was like to see and hear God's messenger in all its heavenly glory. After all, the Bible indicates that angels are not flesh and blood and are most often invisible to humans. The Bible also portrays angelic visitations as stunning occurrences, so glorious and impressive that they amaze and terrify those who see them.

We do know, however, that the Lord God chose the lowest class of people to hear the highest of announcements. We know that the whole world had been waiting thousands of years for the news that God's promised Savior had come. And we know that this message is as profound for us today as it was for the shepherds who "shook in their shoes."

May God bless you and your child as you recall that marvelous message and celebrate our Savior's birth.

The editor

Star of Wonder

The Story of the Wise Men
Matthew 2:1–11 and Luke 2:1–18, and
Numbers 24:17 and Revelation 22:16,
for children

Written by Cynthia A. Hinkle
Illustrated by Johanna van der Sterre

71

Long, long ago, Christmas had no snow;
Folks wore flowing robes and sandals.
In a land of spices, cinnamon, and rice,
People rode donkeys and camels.

But the folks, you see, were like you and me.
They were sinful, mean, and hurting.
Like us they sighed, like us they cried.
We all need God's love and forgiving.

So God had a plan that was bold and grand.
He would send us a loving Savior
To old Bethlehem. To point to Him,
God lit the bright Star of Wonder.

A state's decree counting folks 1-2-3
Brought Mary and Joseph to town.
In the small city, a place not pretty,
Love's perfect, sweet starlight came down.

Happy and weepy, Mary, quite sleepy,
Placed sweet Baby in a hay nest.
Jesus, the Newborn, was safe and warm.
Now, perhaps, Mom can rest.

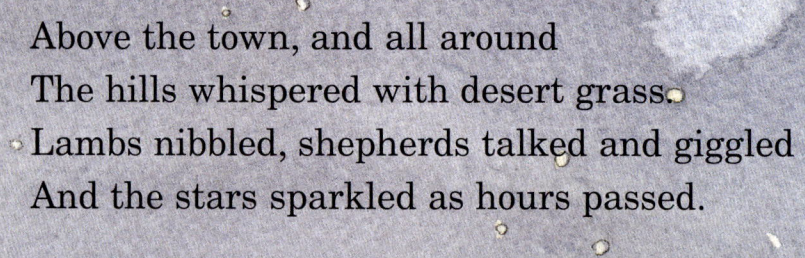

Above the town, and all around
The hills whispered with desert grass.
Lambs nibbled, shepherds talked and giggled
And the stars sparkled as hours passed.

On Bethlehem fields, the shepherds kneeled,
Each shaking in wonder and fright.
Perfect and clear, bright, shiny, and near,
God's glory filled up the night.

There wasn't a doubt, an angel did shout,
"Do not be afraid! It's good news!
There's a new Baby Boy who brings great joy
For everyone, even for you!

"In King David's town, cloth wrapped around
In a manger your Savior lies."
To which angel throngs in the sky sang songs,
"Glory, glory to God on high!"

The angels took flight, still went the night
As the shepherds started to run.
"Off to Bethlehem. Let's race! Let's see Him!
Let's see what our Lord God has done!"

So guests came gawking, telling and talking
Of the Baby—an amazing story!
The skies afire as angel choirs
Sang, "He's the Savior, God's Glory!"

Mary wiped her eyes, their news no surprise;
An angel had already told her.
Son of God is He, mighty King He'll be,
On the throne He'll rule forever.

Months later, at home, how Jesus had grown!
He was crawling all over the floor.
He heard camels bray as He gurgled away
When some Wise Men came to the door.

From afar these men came and by the same
Star of wonder, caravanned to the west.
On the shifting sands, sky maps in hand,
Many miles they marched on their quest.

Then while Mary looked, to Jesus each took
Gifts of myrrh, frankincense, and gold;
For old, old rolls of written paper scrolls
To them the King's birth had foretold.

Born in a stall, Jesus Christ came so small,
The humble, yet great Lord and King.
He lived, died, then rose to save all from sins' woes.
We're forgiven, with life free and lasting!

Lord, help us tell, You are Emmanuel,
God with us, Christ Jesus, You are.
Through true stories, by grace Your glories
Shine for us, for all, like the star!

Dear Parents,

"And we have the word of the prophets made more certain, and you will do well to pay attention to it, as to a light shining in a dark place, until the day dawns and the morning star rises in your hearts." (1 Peter 1:19)

At last the Light had come! The shepherds looked to the sky, heeded the angels' announcement, and came to see. The Wise Men looked to the sky, followed the star, and came to worship. Even wicked Herod took the sign seriously and did what he could to lessen the impact of this new King.

At last the Light had come! After centuries of waiting, the prophecies of the Messiah were fulfilled. God's promised Savior had come, offering forgiveness, peace, and boundless hope to the sin-darkened world. *"Jesus spoke to them, saying, 'I am the light of the world. Whoever follows Me will not walk in darkness, but will have the light of life'"* (John 8:12).

After reading *Star of Wonder* to your child, point out stars around you: Christmas decorations, designs on wrapping paper, and in the night sky. Tell your child that every time we see a star, we can remember the one that led the Wise Men to the Christ Child. Christ is the Star of salvation, announced by Old Testament prophets, that brought eternal light into our world. If your child is old enough, sing together an Epiphany hymn such as "As with Gladness Men of Old" or "Songs of Thankfulness and Praise."

The Editor

My Merry Christmas

ARCH® BOOK

Luke 2:1–20 for children

Written by Theresa Olive
Illustrated by Nancy Munger

So Mary and Joseph of Nazareth,
A town in Galilee,
Traveled down to Bethlehem
To obey the king's decree.

Crowds of other visitors
Stayed there in Bethlehem.
The tired couple tried to find
A place with room for them.

At last, the owner of an inn
Said, "If the two of you don't mind,
You can sleep out in my barn—
It's the only place you'll find."

In the stable, God's own Son,
Named Jesus, soon was born.
Mary wrapped Him up and laid Him
In the manger's hay so warm.

Meanwhile shepherds watched their sheep
Near Bethlehem that night.
An angel suddenly appeared—
The shepherds shook with fright!

The angel said, "Fear not! I bring
Good news for everyone:
A baby's born in Bethlehem—
Your Savior, God's own Son!"

All at once a multitude
Of angels filled the sky,
Shining brighter than the sun
And praising God most high!

The shepherds raced to Bethlehem
And found the baby boy,
Wrapped up in His manger bed.
Their hearts were filled with joy!

The shepherds soon had spread the word
To people far and near:
"Good News! Our Savior has been born!
The Son of God is here!"

Today we still can celebrate,
In many special ways
The time when Jesus Christ was born
And slept in manger hay.

At Christmas when you decorate

Your tree with bright _____ lights,
(favorite color)

They twinkle like the stars that shone
On Bethlehem that night.

When carolers sing "_____,"
(favorite carol)
    And you sing along,
        You're bringing praise to God above
        Just like the angels' song.

Before you eat your Christmas meal
Of ——————————— that tastes so good,
      (favorite food)
Thank God for His blessings,
Like your home and friends and food.

As you open gifts like ———————————,
Or games you like to play,
      (favorite gift)
Think of the gift God gave us
On that very first Christmas Day.

Christmas is a special day,
A time when we recall
The birthday of God's only Son—
The greatest gift of all!

The Arch® Book Bible Story Library

Bible Beginnings

59-1577	The Fall into Sin
59-1534	The First Brothers
59-2206	A Man Named Noah
59-1511	Noah's 2-by-2 Adventure
59-1560	The Story of Creation
59-2239	Where Did the World Come From?

The Old Testament

59-1502	Abraham's Big Test
59-2244	Abraham, Sarah, and Isaac
59-2229	Daniel and the Lions
59-1559	David and Goliath
59-1593	David and His Friend Jonathan
59-2220	Deborah Saves the Day
59-1543	Elijah Helps the Widow
59-2251	Ezekiel and the Dry Bones
59-1567	The Fiery Furnace
59-1570	God Calls Abraham . . . God Calls You!
59-1587	God Provides Victory through Gideon
59-1523	God's Fire for Elijah
59-1542	Good News for Naaman
59-2223	How Enemies Became Friends
59-2247	Isaac Blesses Jacob and Esau
59-1538	Jacob's Dream
59-1539	Jericho's Tumbling Walls
59-2246	Jonah, the Runaway Prophet
59-1514	Jonah and the Very Big Fish
59-2233	Joseph, Jacob's Favorite Son
59-2216	King Josiah and God's Book
59-1583	The Lord Calls Samuel
59-2219	Moses and the Bronze Snake
59-1607	Moses and the Long Walk
59-2266	The Mystery of the Moving Hand
59-1535	A Mother Who Prayed
59-2249	One Boy, One Stone, One God
59-2253	Queen Esther Visits the King
59-2211	Ruth and Naomi
59-1600	Samson
59-1586	The Ten Commandments
59-1608	The Ten Plagues
59-2263	The Tower of Babel
59-1550	Tiny Baby Moses
59-1530	Tried and True Job
59-2260	The 23rd Psalm
59-1603	Zerubbabel Rebuilds the Temple

The New Testament

59-1580	The Coming of the Holy Spirit
59-2259	The Great Commission
59-2207	His Name Is John
59-1532	Jailhouse Rock
59-1520	Jesus and the Family Trip
59-1588	Jesus Calls His Disciples
59-2215	Jesus Shows His Glory
59-1521	Mary and Martha's Dinner Guest
59-2227	Paul's Great Basket Caper
59-2267	The Pentecost Story
59-1578	Philip and the Ethiopian
59-1601	Saul's Conversion
59-1574	Timothy Joins Paul
59-2222	Twelve Ordinary Men
59-1599	Zacchaeus

Arch® Book Companions

59-2232	The Fruit of the Spirit
59-1609	God, I've Gotta Talk to You
59-1575	The Lord's Prayer
59-1562	My Happy Birthday Book

Christmas Arch® Books

59-1579	Baby Jesus Is Born
59-1544	Baby Jesus Visits the Temple
59-1553	Born on Christmas Morn
59-2261	The Christmas Angels
59-1605	The Christmas Message
59-2225	The Christmas Promise
59-1546	Joseph's Christmas Story
59-1499	Mary's Christmas Story
59-1584	My Merry Christmas Arch® Book
59-2252	Oh, Holy Night!
59-1537	On a Silent Night
59-2243	Once Upon a Clear Dark Night
59-2234	The Shepherds Shook in Their Shoes
59-1594	Star of Wonder
56-2209	When Jesus Was Born

11/2013

Easter Arch® Books

59-1551	Barabbas Goes Free
59-2205	The Centurion at the Cross
59-1516	The Day Jesus Died
59-2213	The Easter Gift
59-2221	The Easter Stranger
59-1602	The Easter Victory
59-2265	From Adam to Easter
59-1582	Good Friday
59-1585	Jesus Enters Jerusalem
59-1561	Jesus Returns to Heaven
59-2248	John's Easter Story
59-1592	Mary Magdalene's Easter Story
59-1564	My Happy Easter Arch® Book
59-2258	The Gardens of Easter
59-2231	The Resurrection
59-1517	The Story of the Empty Tomb
59-1504	Thomas, the Doubting Disciple
59-1501	The Very First Lord's Supper
59-1541	The Week That Led to Easter

Miracles Jesus Performed

59-1531	Down through the Roof
59-1568	Get Up, Lazarus!
59-1604	The Great Catch of Fish
59-1581	Jesus Calms the Storm
59-1598	Jesus' First Miracle
59-2230	Jesus Heals Blind Bartimaeus
59-2255	Jesus Heals the Man at the Pool
59-2236	Jesus Heals the Centurion's Servant
59-2226	Jesus Wakes the Little Girl
59-1597	Jesus Walks on the Water
59-1558	A Meal for Many
59-2212	The Thankful Leper
59-1510	What's for Lunch?

Parables and Lessons of Jesus

59-2257	Jesus and the Canaanite Woman
59-1589	Jesus and the Woman at the Well
59-1500	Jesus Blesses the Children
59-1595	Jesus, My Good Shepherd
59-2245	Jesus Teaches Us Not to Worry
59-1540	Jesus Washes Peter's Feet
59-2264	The Lesson of the Tree and its Fruit
59-1606	The Lost Coin
59-2235	The Parable of the Ten Bridesmaids
59-2218	The Parable of the Lost Sheep
59-2224	The Parable of the Prodigal Son
59-2262	The Parable of the Seeds
59-2210	The Parable of the Talents
59-2254	The Parable of the Woman and the Judge
59-2250	The Parable of the Workers in the Vineyard
59-1512	The Seeds That Grew and Grew
59-1503	The Story of Jesus' Baptism and Temptation
59-1596	The Story of the Good Samaritan
59-2214	The Widow's Offering
59-2208	The Wise and Foolish Builders